About the author:

Giridhara Raam is a cybersecurity analyst and GDPR researcher with expertise in unified endpoint management. His articles have helped IT pros understand IT security trends by addressing topics like cybersecurity, DevOps, ransomware, malware, and more. His continued involvement in IT security research includes gathering and sharing knowledge

I0477986

Introduction:

Organizations around the world are moving towards more vigilance in enterprise security. According to Gartner, a leading IT research firm, businesses spent around $86.4 billion on information security (a subset of cybersecurity) in 2017, and that number is expected to hit $93 billion in 2018. Cybercrime research firm Cybersecurity Ventures has also predicted cybersecurity damages could reach $1 trillion between 2017 and 2021, and is expected to reach $6 trillion annually after 2021.

Considering these damages, IDC, a market research firm, states that 70 percent of data breaches begin with endpoints; this illustrates the importance of securing and safeguarding your endpoints—from servers to remote mobile devices—to keep your network safe from cyberattacks and secure the data stored in those endpoints.

About this book:

Securing endpoints to improve IT security introduces you to topics like effective unified endpoint management, overcoming endpoint management challenges, mitigating ransomware and malware, and securing personal data to achieve and sustain GDPR compliance. You'll learn how to manage a heterogeneous network from one central location. You'll also learn about some endpoint security best practices for keeping attackers at bay.

In short, this book will assist you in effectively securing all your endpoints to keep your data and network safe.

Table of contents

deployment and troubleshooting
- Single console for diversified IT security

Chapter 3: Avoiding ransomware, malware, and remote code executions

- Need for automated patch management
- Rolling back patches
- Deploying customized configurations for unique security handling

Chapter 4: Securing personal data and maintaining user privacy

- Inbound and outbound data flow analysis
- Data management, protection, and security
- Managing personal data on desktops
- Managing personal data on mobile devices

Chapter 5: Eight best practices for effective endpoint security

- 1. Automated patch management
- 2. Script deployment
- 3. IT asset management
- 4. User and group privilege management
- 5. Firewall and browser configuration
- 6. BYOD device management
- 7. Mobile application management (MAM)
- 8. Data management life cycle
- The answer is a UEM solution

Chapter 1

Understanding the compelling need for unified endpoint management (UEM)

Thanks to advances in enterprise mobility, employees often use two devices for their official work-related operations. Research firm Enterprise Management Associates states, "roughly half of all workers use [...] both a mobile device and a PC in considering a typical day at [the] office."

Unified endpoint management (UEM) is an IT management technique that typically takes existing mobile device management (MDM) practices and adds other devices, like desktops and laptops, into a consolidated management scope. Effective (UEM) practices can help you take care of all the devices existing both inside and outside your network, all from one location. With new advances in technology emerging each day, the importance of keeping your network devices secure continues to grow exponentially every year; with proper unified endpoint management, you can tackle this never-ending responsibility with confidence.

UEM establishes simplified endpoint complexity

Many organizations' IT environments are compiled of machines in varying departments that work on different operating systems and have their own applications and security configurations.

Depending on the demands of each department, a system will have varying levels of security risks associated with it. For example, the HR department may only work with a few applications, but the product development teams will use multiple tools and applications that not only require constant updates, but must stay up and running to facilitate productivity throughout the entire enterprise. Whether your enterprise is running a single operating system or a combination of several different ones, adopting a UEM solution can provide cut costs, bolstered productivity, and centralized management..

Currently the scope of endpoint management covers servers, desktops, laptops, smartphones, tablets, iPads, and Internet of Things (IoT) devices. A UEM solution can simplify how these various endpoints are managed and secure all heterogeneous user devices from one central location. With all that said, effective endpoint management, when looped into your existing IT service management (ITSM) and IT operations management (ITOM) practices, can produce impressive results.

Note: When the key to all your devices is in one place, you need the right formula to ensure data security and safety. Patching and whitelisting should be your first steps of defense, which will help you avoid most cyber threats. According to a study by research firm Voke Media, of the 318 companies examined, more than 80 percent of breaches occurred due to outdated operating systems and application patches that had been pending for over a year.

The same study found that 27 percent of surveyed companies reported a failed audit in the prior 18 months, of which 81 percent could have been prevented with a patch or configuration change. Similarly, 26 percent reported a breach, of which 79 percent could have been prevented by those same two measures.

UEM drives seamless IT security

Users are constantly making changes to information through their devices, whether it's on laptops or smartphones. In this era of evolving IT environments, you need firm control over user devices, regardless of their location. Most cyberattacks exploiting operating system and application vulnerabilities can be avoided by deploying patches over the internet, without waiting for remote devices to reach your enterprise network. Patching, combined with flexible configurations and deployment capabilities, will drive seamless security for your network.

Remember: In 2017, WannaCry ransomware wrecked havoc around the world, infecting hundreds of thousands of computers across the globe. This outbreak was traced back to a known vulnerability in Windows computers called EternalBlue, which WannaCry exploited. Companies that failed to patch EternalBlue after the WananaCry outbreak also faced the risk of Petya and NotPetya ransomware a few months later.

UEM improves productivity and keeps users happy

With all the applications and operating systems that are updated and monitored centrally, users will spend less time concentrating on application level security, allowing them to focus their attention on other aspects of their jobs. UEM keeps endpoints up and running, which eliminates downtime and helps employees reach project deadlines without any technological hiccups.

Technical stuff: Regardless of the number of endpoints checking in and out of your network each day, you're responsible for keeping your security gateways safe from intruders. Managing a heterogeneous environment by deploying security configurations for applications, firewalls, browsers, and hardware can reduce security risks exponentially. For instance, a simple firewall configuration to disable SMBv1 and port 445 could have prevented the EternalBlue exploit, leaving WannaCry stuck within a single, infected system.

UEM facilitates better business decisions

Understanding user behavior will not only help business decision makers formulate strategies that will help strengthen their IT security and improve employee productivity, but it will also help them better direct their investments. UEM gives you a bird's-eye view of your IT environment; it provides you with proper reporting capabilities, allowing you to make better business decisions, like whether you should purchase new hardware and software, renew applications, and more. With improved visibility, you can formulate a better IT management strategy—which leads to a better business.

Technical stuff: Usage stats come in handy when determining whether or not you have enough licenses for the commercial software used in your network. It's important to track things like the number of devices using each software, as well as the number of times each software is being used and for how long. If you discover that you're not actively using all the licenses you've purchased, you can save money by not renewing those extra licenses.

Chapter 2

Challenges in managing endpoints

2018 has continued the trend of organizations improving employee productivity by providing them mobile devices, with smartphones, chromebooks, and tablets already dominating work culture. Managing all these endpoints from one spot can be convenient, but only if the challenges surrounding endpoint management are handled in an effective way. This chapter introduces a few major challenges every IT department faces when moving towards a more mobile workforce.

Mobile workforce

Each organization's culture varies from the next; likewise, the devices existing in an organization's environment differ for each department. Economics runs on the principle of supply and demand; successfully supplying a market's demands will result in profitable business. That philosophy can apply to IT department as well—if you supply your IT department with the tools they need to effectively perform tasks, you'll see more efficient work from their department, which will, in turn, free them up to work on other, more pressing matters.

Remember: Desktops, laptops, smartphones, tablets, and IoT devices all can be breached into one way or another if their security layers are not properly scrutinized. As more devices are added to an enterprise's network, the likelihood of that network falling victim to an attack increases.

Something to consider: IT security begins with endpoints. Most high-alert security breaches are avoidable with secure and well guarded endpoints.

Managing multiple architectures

Many organizations are compiled of different devices ranging from old, outdated OSs like Windows XP to the more recent, like Chrome OS. Effectively securing all these devices in a central location marks a huge milestone for security professionals. Enterprises that fail to reach this milestone are still highly vulnerable to cyberattacks and zero-day exploits.

Windows, Mac, and Linux management

Each operating system comes with its own pros and cons; Windows comes with better developer compatibility, Mac offers designer harmony, and Linux excels with server adaptability. But it's the IT administrator who has to unify different operating systems—this is where an endpoint management tool comes in handy.

Technical stuff: A UEM solution that supports multiple Linux distributions, with support for virtual machines and hypervisors, can facilitate server management. With support for both Windows and Mac, you'll feel simply tickled pink.

Third-party application management

Organizations often have many different third-party applications that require innovation and dependability. From business meeting software like Skype to document applications like Adobe, third-party application software has proven its worth for most enterprises. Managing all these different, complex, new, and obscure third-party applications from a single console can fix zero-day exploits and prevent remote code executions.

Technical stuff: Browsers are some of the most used third-party applications, making them one of the biggest doorways for an attacker to breach. Neglecting updates on these applications leaves attackers with an open door to your network. Fireball, an adware that took down browsers during July 2017, affected more than 250 million computers worldwide. With the right third-party application management procedure in place, this and similar outbreaks could've been avoided by updating the vulnerable browsers and deploying remote scripts to the machines for complicated threat or vulnerability handling.

Android, iOS, and Windows device management

A growing trend among enterprises is the adoption of a bring your own device (BYOD) policy. With users switching between public networks and corporate networks, securing the data stored on their BYOD devices from the tide of malware and man-in-the-middle attacks has never been more important. A unified endpoint management system can bring mobile devices running on Android, iOS, and Windows within your enterprise's management reach.

Tip: With UEM, you can transfer confidential documents between employee devices, whitelist apps that can exist on your employees' devices, identify lost or stolen employee devices, and wipe corporate data in remote devices.

Demand for proactive security

Gartner has stated "Through 2020, 99% of vulnerabilities exploited will continue to be ones known by security and IT professionals for at least one year." When considering this projected statistic, the idea of ignoring patches and updates sounds downright irrational. In 2017, a string of major ransomware attacks, including WannaCry and NotPetya, exploited unpatched computers, resulting in billions of dollars in damages. And the infamous Meltdown and Spectre vulnerabilities from early 2018 places nearly every computer running a modern processor at risk, unless properly patched. These examples alone should be enough of a reason to strengthen your network security and begin deploying patches on time.

Handling user requests with remote deployment and troubleshooting

It's highly unlikely that you'll be able to physically access all your network's devices for troubleshooting, especially with the growth enterprises experience each year. You need to be able to remotely troubleshoot systems, fulfill remote deployment requests, run scripts remotely, and other tasks from a central location, regardless of whether the devices are on a LAN or WAN. Remote troubleshooting keeps SLA resolutions times low by enabling multiple requests to be handled quickly. With proper remote control capabilities in place, enterprises can fix nearly any issue from anywhere.

Single console for diversified IT security

IT security is a never-ending process. Efficient IT security requires effective handling of different ITSM and ITOM dependencies. You can either employ different procedures to handle this, or try using a product that has good integration capabilities. If you're able to look into tickets and resolve any IT operation-related issues from a single console, your productivity will improve, thereby reducing SLA resolution times.

Technical stuff: Resolving issues related to troubleshooting, deploying software to remote devices, and restarting or shutting down computers remotely, all from your ticket window, can be *especially* handy. You should also utilize one-click access to multiple device management capabilities and combine ITSM and ITOM together to get a complete ITIL implementation.

Chapter 3

Avoiding ransomware, malware, and remote code execution

Cyberattacks happen everywhere on a daily basis. How can you prevent data theft from ransomware, malware, or trojan attacks? What security measures can keep these threats at bay? This section will touch on some real-time malware prevention measures, which will work for future threats.

Need for automated patch management

The Common Vulnerabilities and Exposures (CVE) system recorded 14,712 vulnerabilities in 2017, and just three months into 2018, there have already been over 3,000 vulnerabilities recorded. Considering the number of vulnerabilities discovered every year, enterprises need to identify vulnerabilities in their environment and periodically patch to avoid foreseeable disasters caused by malware, ransomware, or remote code executions exploiting vulnerabilities.

With diversified operating systems and applications, enterprises need to ensure all the different type of vulnerabilities are updated in a timely manner, with proper testing and approval status. But doing this manually is a never-ending and near-impossible task. This is where automated patch management comes in handy. Everything from detection, downloading, testing, and deploying patches—the entire patch management cycle—should be automated.

Remember: Even after patching all your OSs and applications, you are still vulnerable to zero-day attacks, which are essentially impossible to predict and avoid. Automatic patching can resolve zero-day exploits as soon as a patch is made available.

Rolling back patches

While deploying patches can reduce the threat of cyberattacks, it can also become a headache for IT admins when vendors do not properly test the patches they release. Things like performance issues can crop up if a patch is hastily made available before its affects have been properly vetted. Should these problems arise, IT administrators need to be able to roll back ineffective patches once they're identified to reverse any changes that disrupt normal business functions.

Technical stuff: Intel released fixes for Meltdown and Spectre several days after the vulnerabilities were reported. These patches worked well on Meltdown, but Spectre's initial patch release resulted in negative impacts on performance, even causing some systems to crash. This is where rolling back patches comes in handy.

Deploying customized configurations for unique security handling

Though most security procedures can be reinforced with proper patch management, there are certain security threats that require a more customized fix. Beyond application patching, there's still firewall configurations, user privilege management, and file and data management to consider. A single UEM solution can assist with this wide scope of unique security requests that threaten your network.

Remember: You can prevent unwanted adware and spyware by monitoring user devices, allowing those devices to only browse a limited set of websites and restricting their ability to browse websites outside of that whitelist. Fireball, for instance, could have been avoided if proper browser management was in place.

Tip: Redefining your firewall based on your enterprise's specific security needs can keep unwanted traffic out of your network. For example, the EternalBlue vulnerability was mitigated by blocking the vulnerable ports in network devices.

Technical stuff: Not all devices in your network should have access to all data. Defining user and group privileges can limit users' access to data, preventing data loss or theft.

Chapter 4

Securing personal data and maintaining user privacy

Organizations are comprised of huge amount of data; keeping track of all this data by monitoring and securing it is an enormous task. In order to manage this data, you need to sort out inbound flow, storage location, duration of storage, protection, and security measures as well as classify available data and outbound flow. Finally, determining a data retention and deletion period will offer high-level support for data management.

Inbound and outbound data flow analysis

Data flows through corporate networks via the internet and can include email, chats, cloud storage, and sharing, as well as physical and internal means including USB devices and mapped network drives or network shares. With the right data filtering capabilities, organizations will retain only known, essential data inside their networks.

Tip: Limit access to confidential documents by configuring your browsers to be restricted to specific websites, configuring your firewall to limit traffic flow, restricting and limiting your USB devices to avoid data transfer, and redefining user privileges.

Data management, protection, and security

Once data enters an organization, it's the IT security team's responsibility to keep that data intact without allowing a breach or leak. With the right tools, you can identify the network loopholes attackers will exploit to breach your data. There are common and easy touch points for attackers, including unchanged passwords, weak passwords, downloadable mail attachments, BYOD devices, and unpatched or outdated applications. Effectively handling all these loopholes in a timely manner can help keep attackers at bay.

Technical stuff: Identify unchanged user passwords and local user accounts that exist in a system; define file and folder permissions to limit users' scope of accessible documents. Configuring user and group restriction can also help with data protection and access.

Managing personal data on desktops

Information shared by end users is stored in computers and servers; this information is stored in different containers based on where the data is collected from, the type of data, and the need for the data that is collected. To gain control over data stored in computers and servers, data management officers must identify the amount and type of data entering their network, where it's stored, and how it exits the network. Practices like monitoring USB devices, firewalls, browsers, and mapped network drives can help you scrutinize this information and secure corporate data.

Something to think about: Remote code execution can steal data from user machines; with proper security against vulnerabilities , enterprises can avoid remote code execution, as well as data theft.

Managing personal data on mobile devices

In the realm of digital transformation, the world is experiencing major changes due to increased use of mobile and IoT devices. With enterprises moving toward more mobile workforces, keeping employee devices secured from cyberthreats is going to become more challenging and time consuming. Enterprises who adopt a BYOD policy face greater difficulties surrounding mobile deice management, considering that personal data will undoubtable be stored on these devices.

Proper management of mobile devices requires enterprises to differentiate between corporate and personal information. Beyond that, regardless of it's a BYOD or corporate-owned device, you should manage mobile applications, limit unwanted apps from accessing sensitive information by blacklisting them, identify devices that have been jail broken, and take mobile security actions immediately to avoid data theft. You can also make sharing emails and documents more secure with conditional Exchange access and content management capabilities. With the right MDM (or UEM) solution, enterprises can secure personal data on mobile devices.

Tip: Defining role-based access control can help you hand pick which technicians can access which devices.

Remember: Lost or stolen devices place corporate data at risk. With MDM in place, you can locate lost devices geographically and even keep sensitive data secure by remotely wiping corporate data on devices that can't be recovered.

Chapter 5

Eight best practices for effective endpoint security

Enterprise IT security can be maintained with healthy endpoints
. To ensure your endpoints are safe and secure, you need to
apply several industry-defined best practices, which will set the
stage for proper endpoint security.

With so many touch points, it's important to map the right
security controls with the right tools.

Improve your enterprise's endpoint security by following these
eight best practices:

1. Automated patch management

Patching is a security procedure that every enterprise should
practice to avoid unforseen vulnerabilities. With diversified
operating systems and department-specific third-party
applications existing inside your network, there's a good chance
you could fall victim to a zero-day attack; with automated
patching in place, these loopholes can be taken care of in a
timely manner before an attacker can exploit them.

2. Script deployment

Not all application issues can be dealt with using an automated patch management procedure; some issues have to be fixed by remotely deploying custom scripts to machines. Custom scripts give you an extra hand in support when regular patch management procedures aren't enough.

3. IT asset management

With so many different computers, software, and devices existing inside your network, you to be able to see when a device enters or exits your network. With a bird's-eye view over your IT assets, you'll be able to approve and reject devices at a glance, based on their necessity.

4. User and group privilege management

Not all users and groups require access to all documents; defining document privileges to a select number of users and groups can help keep data safe and avoid data loss through unknown sources. Role-based access control for mobile devices can limit data usage by technicians in BYOD devices.

5. Firewall and browser configuration

Browsers are a primary entry point for data to flow into a network. Control browsers in a network by preventing users from visiting unknown or prohibited sites, which can help regulate what kind of data enters through browsers. Regulating browsers can also help prevent malware or adware from entering the network. Firewalls, on the other hand, can help control traffic in the network by defining the ports that are allowed for communications, which can prevent data flow through undefined firewalls.

6. BYOD device management

With mobility and digital transformation driving the future of enterprise workplaces, employees are now using both laptops and smartphones for their day-to-day work routines. You need control over BYOD devices to properly handle personal and corporate data on these devices.

7. Mobile application management (MAM)

Outdated mobile apps and inappropriate apps can cause chaos in an enterprise if their vulnerabilities are exploited by an attacker. With proper MAM procedures in place, you can offer security to users' mobile devices by blacklisting and whitelisting applications. Prohibit desktop applications or block unknown EXEs to avoid any possible remote code executions in the future.

8. Data management life cycle

You should be able to identify data inside your network, at every point in the data management life cycle. This includes identifying the source of data, where it's being stored, how long it's stored, which protection layers it has, and how that data can leave the network. With constant warnings about idle user accounts, idle shared drives, unknown USB devices, and unrecognized software and hardware, you should feel ready to make sure endpoint security is on the right track.

The answer is a UEM solution

A unified endpoint management solution can help your organization achieve all eight of these security best practices and keep your endpoints safe and secure. With so many vendors offering similar capabilities and features in the market, the choice depends on you and your enterprise's unique demands. With a proper evaluation and cost estimation analysis, you can make a choice that will best suit your enterprise.

"Improve your reactive security to identify cyberattacks in time. Maintain your proactive security perimiter to prevent future cyberattacks."

www.ingramcontent.com/pod-product-compliance
Lightning Source LLC
Chambersburg PA
CBHW030041230526
45472CB00002B/618